KU-754-786

Contents

Words in **bold** are in the glossary.

Amazing great white sharks

A great white shark is swimming. It sniffs. It smells a tasty meal. Great white sharks can smell blood that is up to 5 kilometres (3 miles) away. That is just one reason why these sharks are amazing.

Great white sharks are a type of fish. There are more than 450 types of sharks. Great whites are the biggest hunting sharks in the ocean. These sharks eat other ocean animals.

GREAT WHITE SHARKS

by Jaclyn Jaycox

raintree 🍃

a Capstone company — publishers for children

Raintree is an imprint of Capstone Global Library Limited, a company incorporated in England and Wales having its registered office at 264 Banbury Road, Oxford, OX2 7DY – Registered company number: 6695582

www.raintree.co.uk
myorders@raintree.co.uk

Text © Capstone Global Library Limited 2021
The moral rights of the proprietor have been asserted.

All rights reserved. No part of this publication may be reproduced in any form or by any means (including photocopying or storing it in any medium by electronic means and whether or not transiently or incidentally to some other use of this publication) without the written permission of the copyright owner, except in accordance with the provisions of the Copyright, Designs and Patents Act 1988 or under the terms of a licence issued by the Copyright Licensing Agency, Barnard's Inn, 86 Fetter Lane, London, EC4A 1EN (www.cla.co.uk). Applications for the copyright owner's written permission should be addressed to the publisher.

Edited by Mandy Robbins
Designed by Dina Her
Original illustrations © Capstone Global Library Limited 2021
Picture research by Morgan Walters
Production by Tori Abraham
Originated by Capstone Global Library Ltd

978 1 4747 9491 6 (hardback)
978 1 4747 9620 0 (paperback)

British Library Cataloguing in Publication Data
A full catalogue record for this book is available from the British Library.

Acknowledgements
We would like to thank the following for permission to reproduce photographs:
Alamy: Todd Winner, 23; iStockphoto: Pieter De Pauw, 17; Shutterstock: Alessandro De Maddalena, 5, Alexyz3d, 14, Andrea Izzotti, 15, Dominique de La Croix, 7, John Carnemolla, 26, Marc Henauer, 24, Marko Ri, 18, Martin Prochazkacz, 11, Mogens Trolle, 1, 28, Phonix_a Pk.sarote, 27, Ramon Carretero, 25, saulty72, 12, Sergey Uryadnikov, 19, wildestanimal, spread 8-9, 10, Willyam Bradberry, Cover, 20, 21

Every effort has been made to contact copyright holders of material reproduced in this book. Any omissions will be rectified in subsequent printings if notice is given to the publisher.

All the internet addresses (URLs) given in this book were valid at the time of going to press. However, due to the dynamic nature of the internet, some addresses may have changed, or sites may have changed or ceased to exist since publication. While the author and publisher regret any inconvenience this may cause readers, no responsibility for any such changes can be accepted by either the author or the publisher.

Printed and bound in India.

Where great whites live

Great white sharks live in oceans. They are found near South Africa, Australia, New Zealand and the United States. They live in the northern Atlantic and Pacific Oceans too.

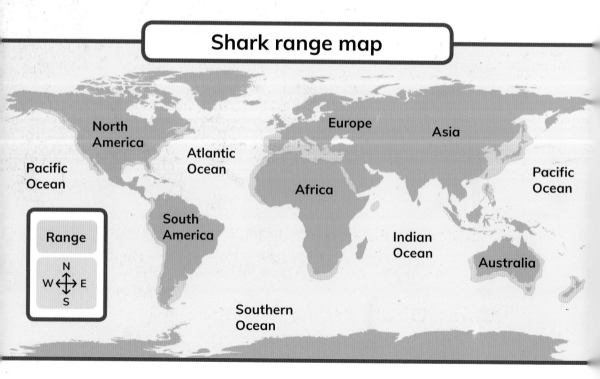

Shark range map

North America

Europe

Asia

Pacific Ocean

Atlantic Ocean

Pacific Ocean

Africa

South America

Indian Ocean

Australia

Range

N
W ◆ E
S

Southern Ocean

Some great white sharks stay near land. They swim near the **coast** all year round. Others move to deeper waters in the winter. They do this to stay warm.

Great white shark bodies

A great white shark gets its name from its white belly. The top of the shark's body is grey. It has blue eyes. Its eyes look black in the water.

Great white sharks are big. They can grow up to 6 metres (20 feet) long. They can weigh up to 2,270 kilograms (5,000 pounds). That's as heavy as a car!

Great white sharks have 300 sharp triangle-shaped teeth that are lined up in rows. Sharp teeth make eating easy. They can eat an animal's skin and bones.

Great white sharks have no bones. Their body frames are made of **cartilage**. This makes the sharks more lightweight. They can swim faster.

dorsal fin

pectoral fin

gills

Great white sharks have long bodies. They have pointed noses. Their shape helps them to swim fast. Great white sharks can swim up to 56 kilometres (35 miles) per hour.

Great whites use fins to steer in the water. They have dorsal fins on their backs. They have two pectoral fins to help them move and turn. They have strong tails that push them ahead.

These sharks also have **gills**. They use them to breathe.

On the menu

A great white shark spots something. It's a seal! The seal is at the surface of the water. The shark speeds towards it. It leaps out of the water. It falls back into the ocean. The seal is in its mouth. The shark has caught its **prey**!

Sea lions are prey for great white sharks.

Great whites hunt alone. They hunt sea lions, seals and dolphins. They also eat whales. Great whites hunt all over the ocean.

It's hard for prey animals to spot a great white shark. Its white belly looks like sunlight from below.

Great white sharks bite their prey. Then they wait for it to die before eating it.

Sharks don't chew their food. They use their sharp teeth to tear prey. They swallow the chunks whole.

Sharks eat a lot at one time. Sometimes fish are hard to find. The sharks can go a month without eating.

Great white sharks are amazing hunters. Their sense of smell helps them to find food. They can see well in the dark. They can see up to 10 times better than humans.

Great white sharks can sense their prey. They can feel where they are in the water. Their prey might try to hide. But a great white shark will find them.

Great white sharks are warmer than the water around them. Most fish are **cold-blooded**. But great white sharks can raise the **temperature** of their blood. They can live where it may be too cold for other sharks.

Life of a great white

Great white sharks live alone. They only meet up to **mate**. Females usually have 2 to 10 pups at a time. Pups are about 1.5 metres (5 feet) long when they are born. They weigh about 35 kilograms (77 pounds).

A female great white shark does not care for her pups. The pups swim away as soon as they are born.

Pups are born with all their teeth. They can hunt on their own. They eat fish and **rays**. Pups watch out for bigger **predators** such as killer whales.

As they grow, they have fewer enemies. Very few animals eat adult great whites. Great white sharks can live for up to 70 years.

Great white dangers

Humans are the biggest threat to sharks. Sharks can be caught in fishing nets. Hunting sharks is against the law, but some people still do it. The shark fins are used in soup.

Nets are used to keep sharks away from beaches.

Oil and plastics can make ocean water dirty. This can make sharks sick. It can also hurt or kill the animals that sharks eat. Then sharks may not have enough food.

The number of great white sharks is falling. But people are working to help them. Some groups free sharks stuck in nets. They clean up oil and plastic from ocean water. They want to make the ocean safer for sharks and other animals.

Fast Facts

Name: great white shark

Habitat: oceans

Where in the world: North Atlantic Ocean, Pacific Ocean, coastal waters near South Africa, Australia, New Zealand and the western United States

Food: sea lions, seals, dolphins, whales and other sharks

Predators: killer whales, humans

Life span: 70 years

Glossary

cartilage strong, rubbery tissue that connects bones in people and animals

coast land next to an ocean or sea

cold blooded having a body temperature that changes with the surrounding temperature

gills body part on the side of a fish; fish use their gills to breathe

mate join with another to produce young

predator animal that hunts other animals for food

prey animal hunted by another animal for food

ray type of fish with a flat body, large wing-like fins and a thin tail

temperature measure of how hot or cold something is

Find out more

Books
Shark vs Killer Whale (Animal Rivals),
Isabel Thomas (Raintree, 2017)

Sharks (DK findout!), DK (DK Children, 2017)

*Sharks and Other Deadly Ocean Creatures:
Visual Encyclopedia*, DK (DK Children, 2016)

Websites
www.bbc.co.uk/cbbc/watch/p00qch9y
Watch this video of a great white shark.

**www.dkfindout.com/uk/animals-and-nature/fish/
great-white-shark**
Learn more about great white sharks and see one
close up!

Index